To:

_____

From:

_____

God Watches Over You

Philip O. Akinyẹmi

GOD WATCHES OVER YOU
Copyright © 2023 by Philip O. Akinyẹmi

Scripture quotations used in this book are taken from the New King James Version of the Holy Bible. Copyright © 1982 by Thomas Nelson, Inc. Used by permission; The Holy Bible, New International Version®. NIV®. Copyright© 1973, 1978, 1984 by the International Bible Society. Used by permission of Zondervan Publishing House. All rights reserved.

All rights reserved. No part of this book may be reproduced or transmitted in any form or by any means, electronic or mechanical, including photocopying, recording, or by any information storage and retrieval system, without permission in writing from the copyright owner.

Author's Contact Email:
feedmypeople365@gmail.com

ISBN:

Softcover:	978-0-9979238-3-4
Hardcover:	978-0-9979238-4-1
Ebook:	978-0-9979238-5-8

To order additional copies of this book go to:
www.philipakinyemi.com/books

Printed in the United States of America

For my grandchildren and all the Children over the world—each of you is precious in the sight of God.

                                        Philip O. Akinyẹmi

JOSEPH IN THE PIT — Genesis 37

Joseph, the son of Jacob, was a godly young man. He would not join his brethren to do evil. Joseph was born in Jacob's old age, and Jacob loved him more than all his children, so he made him a coat of many colors. Joseph was also a dreamer. He had dreams that his family would one day bow before him. As a result, his brethren hated him more.

One day, his father sent him to go and see his brethren looking after the flock. When his brethren saw him, they planned to kill him, but instead decided to throw him into a pit, and later sold him into slavery. God protected him in the pit and wherever he went. Joseph later became a governor in Egypt, where he saved his people from hunger during a severe famine.

"The angel of the LORD encamps around those who fear Him, and He delivers them" (Psalm 34:7).

MOSES — Exodus 1-2

At the time Moses was born, Pharaoh, the king of Egypt, had made a law to kill any newborn boys of Israel. But Jochebed, his mother, hid him for three months, and when she could no longer hide him, she got a papyrus basket for him and coated it with tar and pitch. Then placed the child in it and laid it in the reeds by the river's bank. His sister Miriam stood at far distance to see what will happen to the child.

God protected the child and did not allow any evil to come to him. Then the king's daughter came to the river to bathe, and there she found him. God wonderfully arranged that the baby should be given back to his mother to raise him for Pharaoh's daughter. When the child grew older, she took him back to Pharaoh's daughter and he became her son. She named him Moses, saying, "Because I drew him out of the water."

"Behold, children are a heritage from the LORD" (Psalm 127:3).

SAMUEL — 1 Samuel 1-2

Samuel's mother Hannah had been barren for a long time, and she prayed that if the Lord gave her a son, she would give the son back to the Lord for His service all the days of his life. The Lord answered her prayer, and Hannah kept her vow. When Samuel was weaned (still a young child), Hannah brought him to the temple in Shiloh to live with Eli the priest, and Samuel remained there. The Lord watched him day and night and preserved him from evil. He grew up to be a great prophet and a leader in Israel.

"I will never leave you nor forsake you" (Hebrews 13:5).

DAVID – 1 Samuel 17

David as a young man kept his father's sheep. A lion came and took a lamb; David fought with the lion and killed it. Another time, a bear came like the lion, and he also killed the bear. God protected him from these dangerous animals. One day, David's father Jesse asked him to take food to his older brothers who were in the army and to see how they were doing. The Israelite army was fighting with the Philistine army.

David heard the Philistine champion Goliath mocking the army of the Lord, and he was sad that someone would say bad things about God's people. David trusted God, who gave him victory over a lion and a bear, to give him victory over Goliath, who was a 9' 9" tall giant. David convinced King Saul that he would fight and defeat Goliath. With his sling and a stone, he approached Goliath and killed him.

"For with God nothing will be impossible" (Luke 1:37).

JOASH – 2 Kings 11

Joash, the infant son of King Ahaziah of Judah, was spared by God when the king was murdered and his mother Athaliah ordered all the members of the royal family to be killed. God watched over Joash and protected him, and Jehosheba, his aunt, hid him from Athaliah for six years while she ruled as queen.

In the seventh year, Joash was anointed and proclaimed king by Jehoiada the priest, for God had promised David that a king would never be wanting from his lineage.

"Not one of all the LORD's good promises to the house of Israel failed" (Joshua 21:45).

THE THREE YOUNG HEBREW MEN — Daniel 3

King Nebuchadnezzar of Babylon made a golden image and asked everyone to bow down and worship it. Anyone who refused would be thrown into a burning furnace. Shadrach, Meshach, and Abednego, three young Hebrew men, refused to worship the idol. They were Jews who had been taught from childhood not to worship an image (idol), but only God. The king was furious and immediately ordered them to be thrown into the furnace. God sent His angel to protect them inside the fire, and it had no power over them because they trusted in God.

"You shall have no other gods before me." "You shall not bow down to them or worship them" (Exodus 20:3, 5).

"When you pass through the waters, I will be with you; and when you pass through the rivers, they will not sweep over you. When you walk through the fire, you will not be burned; the flames will not set you ablaze" (Isaiah 43:2).

DANIEL — Daniel 6

During the reign of king Darius, the Medes, the leaders of the people conspired and made a law to catch Daniel. The decree says, that whoever petitions any god or man for thirty days except king Darius shall be cast into the den of lions. Daniel knew the living God and served Him with his whole heart. Daniel refused to pray to man, and only prayed to his God. They threw Daniel into a den of lions, thinking the lions would eat him up, but God protected him, and the lions could not harm him.

The following day, the king came near the den and called on Daniel, and he answered, "My God sent His angel and shut the lions' mouths, and they have not harmed me, because I was found innocent before Him; and, toward you, O king, I have committed no crime" (Daniel 6:23). The king was very pleased and gave orders for Daniel to be taken up out of the den.

> "Yea, though I walk through the valley of the shadow of death, I will fear no evil; For You are with me; Your rod and Your staff, they comfort me" (Psalms 23:4)

JONAH

Jonah was a prophet of God. The Lord sent him to the great city of Nineveh to preach against it because of its wickedness. Instead of going to Nineveh, Jonah got into a ship going to Tarshih; he was disobedient to the Lord. The Lord sent a great wind on the sea, and the people were afraid that they might all die. They found out that Jonah was the cause for violent storm, so they tossed him into the sea. A big fish came and swallowed up Jonah, but he prayed inside the fish. The Lord forgave him and commanded the fish to vomit him onto dry land after three days. He then went to preach to the people of Nineveh, and they repented.

"Where can I go from your Spirit? Where can I flee from your presence? If I go up to the heavens, you are there; if I make my bed in the depths, you are there" (Psalm 139:7-8).

PETER — Acts 12

King Herod put Peter in prison for preaching the gospel. The church started praying wholeheartedly to God for him. The night before Herod was to bring him to trial, Peter was sleeping between two soldiers, tied with two chains, but an angel of God woke Peter up and asked him to follow him. They left the prison, and when they reached the Iron Gate to the city, it opened by itself.

Peter thought he was dreaming. After the angel led him to the city, he disappeared. Peter then knew it was God who sent His angel to save him. God preserved the life of Peter.

"A righteous man may have many troubles, but the LORD delivers him from them all" (Psalm 34:19).

THEIR ANGELS ARE BEFORE GOD - Matthew 18

Children were brought to Jesus so that He could place His hands on them and bless them. His disciples thought He was too busy and had no time for the children, but Jesus told His disciples not to stop the children from coming to Him.

◇◇

But when Jesus saw it, He was greatly displeased and said to them, "Let the little children come to Me, and do not forbid them; for of such is the kingdom of God." And He took them up in His arms, put His hands on them, and blessed them" (Mark 10:14, 16).

"See that you do not look down on one of these little ones. For I tell you that their angels in heaven always see the face of my Father in heaven" (Matthew 18:10).

◇◇

Psalm 23

¹ The Lord is my shepherd, I lack nothing.

² He makes me lie down in green pastures,
He leads me beside quiet waters,

³ He refreshes my soul. He guides me along the right paths for his name's sake.

⁴ Even though I walk through the darkest valley,
I will fear no evil, for you are with me;
your rod and your staff, they comfort me.

⁵ You prepare a table before me in the presence of my enemies.
You anoint my head with oil; my cup overflows.

⁶ Surely your goodness and love will follow me
all the days of my life, and I will dwell in the house of
the Lord forever

READ DAILY AND PRACTICE SAYING IT OUT LOUD

Psalm 121

1 I lift up my eyes to the hills— where does my help come from?
2 My help comes from the Lord, the Maker of heaven and earth.
3 He will not let your foot slip; He who watches over you will not slumber.
4 indeed, He who watches over Israel will neither slumber nor sleep.
5 The Lord watches over you; the Lord is your shade at your right hand;
6 the sun will not harm you by day, nor the moon by night.
7 The Lord will keep you from all harm— He will watch over your life;
8 the Lord will watch over your coming and going both now and forevermore.

READ DAILY AND PRACTICE SAYING IT OUT LOUD

Puzzle #1

Across

[3] Peter was put in prison for _____ the gospel.

[6] His mother's name was Jochebed.

[7] He was one of the Hebrew young men thrown into the burning furnance.

[8] He later became a governor in Egypt.

[12] They are the heritage of the Lord.

Down

[1] God sent Jonah to preach to the people of _____.

[2] He said, let the little children come to Me and do not forbid them.

[4] The Lord is my _____ I shall not want.

[5] David killed him with a sling and a stone.

[9] The _____ of the Lord shut the lions' mouths from killing Daniel.

[10] She was the mother of Samuel.

[11] He was the king when Daniel was thrown into the lions' den.

Solution: 1. Nineveh, 2. Jesus, 3. Preaching, 4. Shepherd, 5. Goliath, 6. Moses, 7. Shadrach, 8. Joseph, 9. Angel, 10. Hannah, 11. Darius, 12. Children.

Puzzle #2

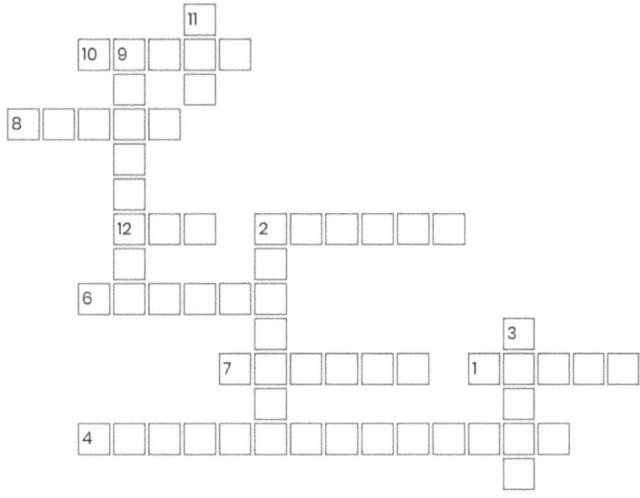

Across

[1] He was seven years old when he became a king in Judah.

[2] She was Moses' big sister.

[4] The king of Babylon who made a golden image and asked everyone to worship it.

[6] Moses was hidden for three ____.

[7] He was thrown into the lions' den for praying to his God.

[8] An angel woke him up while sleeping between two soldiers in the prison.

[10] He was the father of Joseph.

[12] Samuel as a young boy lived with this priest.

Down

[2] He was another Hebrew young man thrown into the burning furnace.

[3] He was in the fish belly for three days.

[9] He was the third Hebrew young man thrown into the burning furnance.

[11] He always watches over you.

Solution: 1. Joash, 2. Miriam, 3. Meshach, 4. Jonah, 5. Nebuchadnezzar, 6. Months, 7. Daniel, 8. Peter, 9. Abednego, 10. Jacob, 11. God, 12. Eli.

Other Books by Philip O. Akinyemi

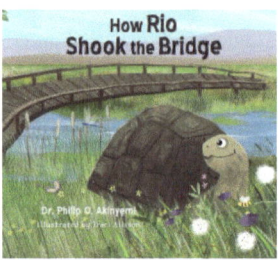

Rio the tortoise was not intimidated and didn't feel inferior keeping company with the elephant, and thereby achieved his desire to shake the bridge. Are you afraid of joining someone who is smarter or better than you? You can accomplish more if you team up with someone better than you.
ISBN: 978-1-7342603-0-4

This book uses some Bible characters who obeyed God and were rewarded or blessed to illustrate the importance of obedience. For example, Noah obeyed God and built an ark, and he and his family were the only ones saved from the flood. If you too obey God, your parents, and those in authority, you will be rewarded. **ISBN: 978-1-7351099-5-4**

An exciting collection of 101 Bible search puzzles with 10 short memory verses and 20 "fill in the blank" verses. Kids will learn about God and His love, protection, provision, salvation, and many other important things. And you will have fun while learning. This puzzle book is great for children ages 6-10, but adults can enjoy it too!
ISBN: 978-1-7351099-78

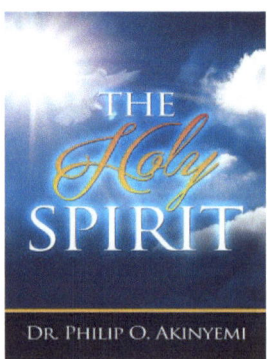

Do you know the Holy Spirit is your loving and faithful Comforter in time of sorrow? He is a divine Person who is available 24/7 to help you. Jesus the Son of God depended utterly upon the Holy Spirit in His earthly ministry, and we must do likewise in order to be effective and successful in our calling in life.
ISBN: 978-1-60383-524-4

www.ingramcontent.com/pod-product-compliance
Lightning Source LLC
Chambersburg PA
CBHW041437010526
44118CB00002B/100